BALTIMORE ™
THE PLAGUE SHIPS

VOLUME ONE

Story by
MIKE MIGNOLA
CHRISTOPHER GOLDEN

Art by
BEN STENBECK

Colors by
DAVE STEWART

Letters by
CLEM ROBINS

Cover Art by
MIKE MIGNOLA with **DAVE STEWART**

Editor SCOTT ALLIE

Associate Editor SAMANTHA ROBERTSON

Assistant Editor DANIEL CHABON

Collection Designer AMY ARENDTS

Publisher MIKE RICHARDSON

DARK HORSE BOOKS ®

For William Hope Hodgson, who had a lot to say about wrecked ships and fungus.
—Mike Mignola

For Gene Colan, the first person to show me that comics could be creepy.
—Christopher Golden

For Danny Cox and Action Man.
—Ben Stenbeck

Mike Richardson *President and Publisher* • Neil Hankerson *Executive Vice President* • Tom Weddle *Chief Financial Officer* • Randy Stradley *Vice President of Publishing* • Michael Martens *Vice President of Book Trade Sales* • Anita Nelson *Vice President of Business Affairs* • David Scroggy *Vice President of Product Development* • Dale LaFountain *Vice President of Information Technology* • Darlene Vogel *Senior Director of Print, Design, and Production* • Ken Lizzi *General Counsel* • Matt Parkinson *Senior Director of Marketing* • Davey Estrada *Editorial Director* • Scott Allie *Senior Managing Editor* • Chris Warner *Senior Books Editor* • Diana Schutz *Executive Editor* • Cary Grazzini *Director of Print and Development* • Lia Ribacchi *Art Director* • Cara Niece *Director of Scheduling*

Special thanks to Jason Hvam and Pasquale Ruggiero

DarkHorse.com

Published by Dark Horse Books
A division of Dark Horse Comics, Inc.
10956 SE Main Street
Milwaukie, OR 97222

First paperback edition: December 2011
Scholastic edition: 2012
ISBN 978-1-61655-044-8

1   3   5   7   9   10   8   6   4   2

Printed at Midas Printing International, Ltd., Huizhou, China

This volume collects the *Baltimore: The Plague Ships* comic-book series,
issues #1–#5, published by Dark Horse Comics.

BACK FROM THE DEAD

by
JOE HILL

1.

LET'S PLAY AN ASSOCIATIVE GAME. Clear your head. I'll drop a word on you, and you say the first thing that comes to mind. Or, if you're reading this graphic novel on a crowded train, you can just whisper to yourself. Ready? Here goes:

Comics.

Mm-hm. You said "Superman," right? Or was it "Batman"? Maybe, just *maybe*, you said, "capes." (Okay, sure, a couple of you out there replied with something ridiculous, like, "onward," just to show how original you are, but trust me, everyone else thought of superheroes.)

I don't know how old you are—you might be fifteen or you might be fifty—but the odds are that the comics you were raised on featured men in ill-advised tights, battling psychotic grotesqueries in the name of truth, justice, and a possible Saturday-morning cartoon. I love cape stories myself, always have. Superman and Batman are more than great characters; they are icons and archetypes, and their stories inform us about ourselves and our historical moment.

Yet we are not too far removed from a period in time when comics were known not for their masked titans, but for their decaying fiends; when they were famous, not for stories of superpowered heroism, but supernatural perversion; not for displays of idealized sacrifice, but for *human* sacrifice. There was a moment when, if we were to play my associative word game, you might've responded to the word "comics" with "horror," or "crime," or "torture," or . . .

. . . tragically . . .

. . . "delinquency." (And yes, probably a few smartasses would've replied with "onward" or some other word that has no relationship to my prompt. But then every generation has its share of smartasses. I have occasionally been accused of being one myself, even by the cowriter of this very comic, Christopher Golden.)

I'm not going to use this space to rehash what happened to horror comics in the 1950s: psychiatrist Fredric Wertham's unscientific study purporting to show a connection between horror comics and sadistic behavior among boys, the shameless kangaroo court put together by Senator Kefauver to attack the comic-book industry (and free speech itself), the creation of the Comics Code, which shoved artists and writers into a superhero-shaped coffin and buried them alive under six feet of hysterical repression. If you want to read about it, I recommend a book titled *The Ten-Cent Plague* by David Hajdu, which methodically documents the effort to eradicate the disease of horror comics in the name of public health . . . the first skirmish in a tiresome culture war that continues to this day.[1]

No, my point is this: if they weren't in such a rush to strangle the life out of the horror comics, the repression brigade might've learned a very valuable lesson from them. The departed—especially those who have suffered a cruel and unjust death—have a nasty way of opening their

---

[1] When an outraged parent writes their newspaper to claim *Grand Theft Auto* or Eminem went and turned their child into a sulky, arrogant teenager, remember two things: (1) children turn into sulky, arrogant teenagers all on their own, without any assist from popular culture, and (2) the irate parent is repeating all the same arguments that were made against horror comics, Elvis, motorcycle movies, and the hula hoop.

eyes and clawing their way out of the soil the moment you turn your back on 'em.

Somewhere in here, when no one was paying attention, horror comics came back from the dead, baby. *Hellboy. Hack/Slash. 30 Days of Night. The Goon. The Walking Dead.*

Baltimore.

Last but not least, *Baltimore*. Unapologetically: *Baltimore*.

2.

Let's say we turned my associative game around. Let's say you suggested a word, and I had to reply, honestly, with the first thing that came into my mind. And then you said, "fun."

My response would depend somewhat on when we played. If this were the fall of 2005, I would've said, "League," thinking of Alan Moore's *League of Extraordinary Gentlemen*. If this were the winter of 2007, I would've said, "Y," mindful of Brian Vaughan's game-changing comic, *Y: The Last Man*. No matter when we played—this year or twenty-five years ago—I probably would have answered with the title of a comic book. They have a lifelong hold on me I can't explain and don't understand. They light up all the pleasure circuits . . . especially the darker comics, those stories of desperate stands against a tide of infection, madness, and the damned.

Here, in the last frozen days of 2010, my high of choice is *Baltimore: The Plague Ships*, one of the most energetic and inventive works on the aforementioned list of remarkable new horror comics.

Plague Ships expands on a story begun in *Baltimore; or, The Steadfast Tin Soldier and the Vampire*, an illustrated novel by Christopher Golden and Mike Mignola, which was itself a thunderous war machine of a book, a relentless bombardment of action and ideas.[2] But don't worry if you haven't read the novel. This comic is not a sequel, but rather a companion, a second doorway into the same shadowy crypt. It introduces us to the grim, tireless, and really exceptionally well-armed Lord Henry Baltimore, and in less than twelve gruesome, violent, and brain-busting pages, his quest to destroy the king vampire named Haigus is *our* quest . . . and never mind that death sits on Lord Baltimore's shoulder "for those who ally themselves with him." We'll have to take our chances.

We can skip the plot summary; you're about to read the thing. Suffice it to say that *Plague Ships* moves forward with the ferocity and drive of its unstoppable protagonist, and throws at you all the visual horrors you would expect of *Hellboy* creator Mike Mignola, and all the mad, stomach-churning concepts that are the stock-in-trade of novelist Christopher Golden. Their vision is made complete by the muscular line work of artist Ben Stenbeck and the moody, chilling colors of Dave Stewart. I could mount a five-thousand-word argument to intellectually defend the excitement I feel for *Plague Ships*. I could drone on about how it operates as a fusion work, blending horror with the sensibility of steampunk sci-fi, to make a new genre (splattersteam?). I could discuss its playful riffs on classic nineteenth-century genre tropes (haunted islands, archaic submarines, Poe's red death).

But truthfully, my response to *Plague Ships* was something I felt more in my nerve endings; it was visceral, not intellectual. Stenbeck, Stewart, Golden, and Mignola had me by the third panel of page 4.

Max really should've run.

Okay. One more word-association game. I get to pick this time.

Ready?

Onward.

Joe Hill
New Hampshire
December 2010

---

[2] It was also, on the level of production design, the most beautiful-looking wide-release novel published in 2007, in any genre. Seriously—this bastard had the quality and beauty of a one-hundred-dollar limited edition. If every hardcover was such a pleasure to read and hold, the e-book industry would be nowheresville.

CHAPTER ONE

VILLEFRANCHE, ON THE COAST OF FRANCE. AUGUST 1916.

HALF A YEAR SINCE THE PLAGUE PUT AN END TO THE WAR, BUT THE DYING GOES ON AND ON.

LORD BALTIMORE'S QUEST CONTINUES.

MAX SHOULD'VE RUN.

BAMM

HURRY, FOOL. THE OTHERS WILL ESCAPE YOU.

SKREEE

NO, DAMN YOU! NOT UNTIL YOU TELL ME WHERE HE IS!

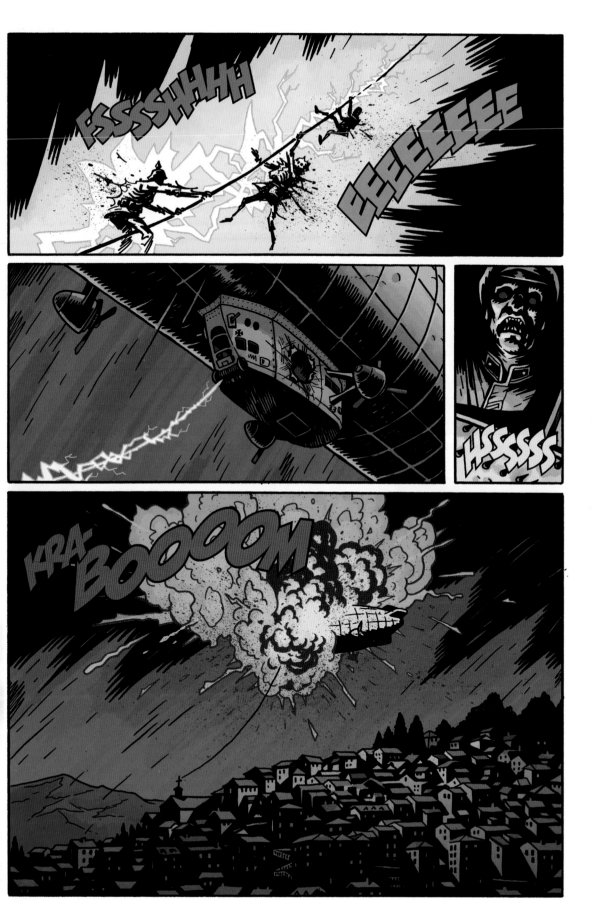

UNGHHH...

THERE, YOU SEE? THE MAN IS GRISTLE. EVEN *HELL* WOULD SPIT HIM OUT.

BACK, WITCH! YOU'LL NOT HAVE ME!

I DON'T *WANT* YOU, FOOL. BUT WATCH YER TONGUE OR I'LL CALL THE LIGHTNING DOWN ON YOU AS I DID ON THE LEECHES.

"CALL THE LIGHTNING"? *LISTEN* TO YOURSELF.

YOU SHOULD THANK ME FOR IT.

COME INTO THE LIGHT!

"...THE MAN JUST SCOURED THE FILTH FROM OUR HOME. THE **LEAST** WE OWE HIM IS THE TRUTH. THE ZEPPELIN CORPS WERE RECENT ARRIVALS, ONLY A FORTNIGHT AGO. **YOUR** VAMPIRE WAS HERE LONG BEFORE THAT.

"THE PLAGUE HAD TOUCHED US **BEFORE** HE CAME, BUT IT SPREAD MUCH MORE QUICKLY AFTER HIS ARRIVAL. HE KILLED MANY, AND OTHERS HE MADE LIKE HIM. TWO NIGHTS AGO A SHIP SAILED FROM HERE BOUND FOR LIVORNO, ON THE ITALIAN COAST. WHISPERS SAY IT SAILED **AFTER DARK** BECAUSE YOUR VAMPIRE WAS ON BOARD."

I'LL NEED A SHIP, THEN. THE SWIFTEST VESSEL AVAILABLE. WHERE CAN I FIND A MAN WILLING TO CARRY ME TO LIVORNO?

NOT ANOTHER **WORD**, GIRL...

"...YOU HAVE TOLD HIM WHAT HE NEEDS TO KNOW.

"THIS VILLAGE HAS BEEN CURSED **ENOUGH**, SIR. WE CAN'T **AFFORD** TO HAVE ANYTHING MORE TO DO WITH YOU."

"DON'T LISTEN TO MY GRAND-MOTHER. I KNOW A MAN WITH A SHIP. I CAN HELP..."

23

24

WHO'S
THERE?

ARE
YOU STILL SO
DETERMINED
TO TRAVEL
ALONE?

29

CHAPTER TWO

"FOR A MOMENT I FEARED YOU MIGHT KILL HIM."

"THE CONSTABLE IS A *FOOL,* VANESSA, BUT HE ISN'T MY ENEMY. I DIDN'T DO HIM ANY PERMANENT DAMAGE."

"NO, BUT HE'LL WAKE WITH QUITE A *HEAD-ACHE--*"

"WELL EARNED."

YOU'LL GET NO ARGUMENT FROM ME, LORD BALTIMORE. I JUST HOPE YOU NEVER HAVE REASON TO THINK OF *ME* AS A FOOL.

FAR TOO LATE FOR THAT. *YOU* WERE A FOOL THE MOMENT YOU JOINED YOUR FATE WITH MINE.

NOW YOU SOUND LIKE MY *GRAND-MOTHER.*

LET'S HURRY. WE WANT TO BE AWAY BEFORE DAWN.

33

39

"FOR *DAYS*, THE WAR IN FRANCE HAD STALLED ON A SINGLE PATCH OF GROUND. I FEARED I WOULD FIGHT THERE *FOREVER*, THAT EVERY MAN IN EUROPE WOULD COME THERE TO DIE.

"AT NIGHT THE *HESSIANS* CAMPED IN THE WOODS ON ONE SIDE, AND OUR FORCES ON THE OTHER, AND *BY DAY* WE SOWED THE EARTH WITH EACH OTHER'S *BLOOD.*

"MY MEN DUG MORE *GRAVES* THAN *TRENCHES.*

"SO WHEN THE WORD CAME DOWN THAT WE HAD BEEN CHOSEN FOR A NIGHTTIME ATTACK, PRACTICALLY A *SUICIDE RUN* INTO THE ENEMY CAMP, MY BOYS *CHEERED.*

"THERE WERE *NO STARS* THAT NIGHT... *NO MOON.*

"WE THOUGHT THE DARK WOULD HIDE US.

"WE WERE *FOOLS*."

DOWN!

41

...UNGHHH...

44

IS SOMEONE THERE?

53

CHAPTER THREE

GOODNESS. WHAT'S **HAPPENED** TO YOU, CAPTAIN?

YOU BE CAREFUL NOW.

YOU'LL CATCH YOUR **DEATH.**

"THE **PLAGUE** HAD BEGUN.

"TRUTHFULLY, I BELIEVE IT BEGAN THE VERY **MOMENT** I WOUNDED THE VAMPIRE. WHEN HE **BLED** INTO THE SOIL WHERE HUNDREDS LAY DYING, THE PLAGUE TOOK **ROOT.**"

HOW DID YOU MANAGE TO **HOLD ON** TO ALL THOSE **WEAPONS** WITHOUT THEM DRAGGING YOU TO THE BOTTOM?

THEY'RE SO MUCH A **PART** OF ME NOW THAT I NEVER FEEL THEIR WEIGHT.

I ONLY WISH I HADN'T LOST MY **RIFLES** AND MY **HARPOON.**

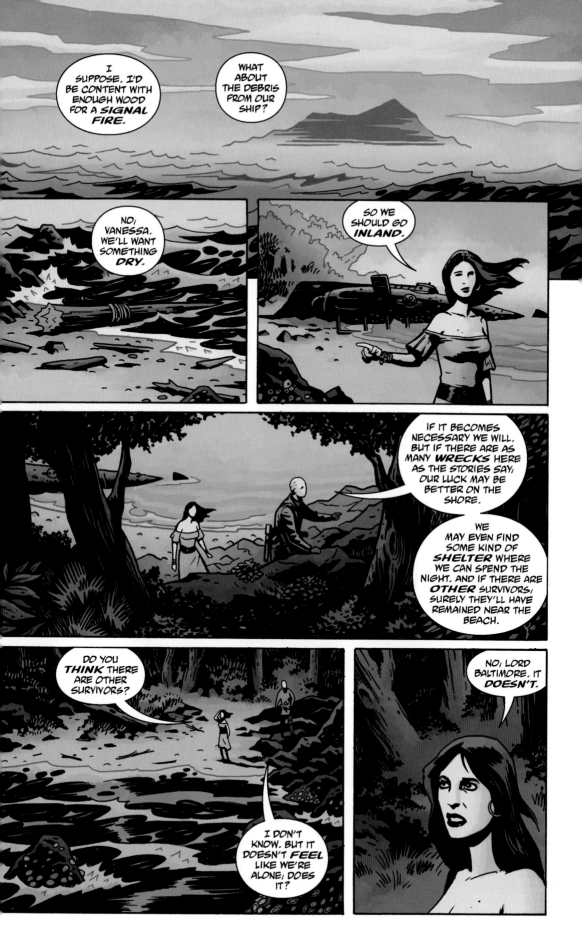

THAT'S **NOT** FROM THE BATTLE OF FURIANI.

IT'S A **PLAGUE** SHIP.

HAVE A LOOK AT *THIS.*

MY LORD! WHAT *IS* IT?

SOME KIND OF *FUNGUS.*

WHERE ARE YOU *GOING?*

STAY HERE.

GLADLY.

MY GOD.

WHAT *IS* IT? SOMETHING TO DO WITH THE *PLAGUE?*

I'VE NEVER SEEN ITS LIKE BEFORE.

PLEASE TELL ME WE'RE DONE HERE.

SKRITCH

CHAPTER FOUR

"I HAD BEEN IN LOVE WITH ELOWEN SINCE WE WERE CHILDREN. WE WED SIX MONTHS BEFORE THE WAR BEGAN.

"YOU KNOW THE HELL I ENDURED ON THE BATTLEFIELD, AND AFTER. YOU KNOW THE THREATS THAT THE SCARRED VAMPIRE HAD MADE.

"THE PLAGUE HAD RAVAGED EUROPE, HALTING THE WAR, AS MEN RUSHED HOME TO BE WITH THOSE THEY LOVED, OR TO DIE WITH THEM. THE VAMPIRES MULTIPLIED. SHADOWS STIRRED. BUT I COULD NOT SHAKE THE FEELING THAT HAIGUS'S WARNING HAD BEEN PERSONAL, THAT HIS WAR WAS WITH *ME*.

"ON THE JOURNEY HOME, I BEFRIENDED THE CAPTAIN OF THE SHIP THAT SAILED ME ACROSS THE CHANNEL...A BRAVE MAN NAMED *DEMETRIUS AISCHROS*.

"I INVITED HIM TO TRAVEL WITH ME. ONLY AFTERWARD DID I REALIZE I WANTED HIS COMPANY BECAUSE I WAS AFRAID OF WHAT I WOULD FIND WHEN I REACHED HOME."

ELOWEN?

"TIME PASSED. SUMMER TURNED TO AUTUMN. AISCHROS HAD TO RETURN TO HIS SHIP. I HAD FALLEN INTO A TERRIBLE STATE, DELIRIOUS WITH FEVER."

"I FELT AS IF I WERE A PUPPET CAST ASIDE BY THE PUPPETEER, THOUGH WHETHER HE HAD BEEN GOD OR THE DEVIL, I DID NOT KNOW."

"I HAD BECOME A HOLLOW MAN."

"AND THAT SICKNESS IS ONE THAT NO DOCTOR CAN CURE."

THANK YOU FOR COMING ALL THE WAY OUT TO THE ISLAND, GENTLEMEN.

WE ARE AT YOUR SERVICE, LADY BALTIMORE. PLEASE DO SUMMON US IF LORD BALTIMORE SHOWS ANY CHANGE, FOR THE BETTER OR FOR THE WORSE.

ELLIE?

BE WITH ME.

COME TO ME, HENRY.

"I HAD SEEN ENOUGH ON MY JOURNEY HOME FROM WAR TO KNOW SHE MIGHT RISE; AND I *WANTED* HER EMBRACE."

...AS I FEARED...

ENOUGH!

DON'T BE A FOOL, LORD BALTIMORE! THIS IS *NOT* YOUR BRIDE. GIVE YOURSELF TO HER AND YOUR SOUL IS *FORFEIT!*

AWAY, FOOL!

"MY SOUL WAS BLACK WITH GRIEF. I WAS ALREADY DEAD INSIDE. WHAT DIFFERENCE IF MY FLESH WERE TO DIE AS WELL?"

IF NOT FOR **YOUR** SOUL, THEN FOR **ELOWEN'S.**

HENRY? DON'T YOU LOVE ME?

I DO. I TRULY DO.

HSSSSSSSSS

HER FLESH BURNS, BUT THE **CREATURE** ISN'T DEAD UNTIL YOU HAVE DESTROYED THE VAMPIRE'S **SOUL** AS WELL.

AWAY FROM ME NOW, MAN OF GOD. IF GOD HAS BROUGHT ALL OF THIS UPON ME, THEN HE IS NO LESS DEVIL THAN THE DEVIL HIMSELF.

YOU ARE MISTAKEN. IT WAS A VISION FROM GOD THAT BROUGHT ME HERE.

YOU ARE NO LESS A WEAPON THAN *THIS*, MY FRIEND. GOD HAS *HONED* YOU WITH HAMMER AND ANVIL. HE HAS MADE YOU SUFFER SO THAT THE WORLD MIGHT BE SPARED FAR WORSE.

"SIX MONTHS AGO, I HAD A VISION WHILE WORKING IN MY GARDEN."

"A VISION OF WHAT?"

"THE RED DEATH."

IT'S COMING, MY FRIEND. AND GOD HAS CALLED YOU TO ARMS AGAINST IT.

AND YOU HAVE BEEN FIGHTING AGAINST THIS RISING EVIL EVER SINCE.

I HAVE BEEN HUNTING THE MONSTER THAT KILLED MY WIFE. THAT IS MY SOLE PURPOSE. IF GOD HAS SOME *OTHER* MISSION, HE MUST FIND HIS *OWN* SOLDIERS.

OR SO I TELL MYSELF.

AND YET I CANNOT HELP FEELING, SO MUCH OF THE TIME, THAT I AM SOME IVORY PAWN, CRUDELY CARVED AND POORLY PLAYED.

BUT SLEEP, NOW, VANESSA. WE'LL BE ALL RIGHT.

THERE ARE NO MORE ENEMIES HERE.

CHAPTER FIVE

"I THINK YOU'VE HEARD ENOUGH OF MY STORY FOR NOW...

"WOULD THAT I COULD RETREAT FROM IT SO EASILY.

"BUT THERE WILL BE NO PEACE FOR ME. NOT EVEN IN SLEEP."

UHHHH...

AHHH...

VANESSA.

"IT IS A *TIME* OF *EVIL*, VANESSA."

THE PLAGUE HAS PLANTED THE SEEDS OF A THOUSAND DREADFUL HARVESTS!

"NOW WE REAP WHAT IT HAS SOWN."

THWAK

"WHAT ABOUT THE REST OF YOUR FAMILY. WERE THEY...?"

TAINTED?

OH, YES. HAIGUS HAD WAITED FOR MY RETURN BEFORE HE MURDERED MY WIFE AND TRANSFORMED HER INTO A FIEND. HE WANTED ME TO WITNESS THAT...

"...BUT HE HAD DEFILED THEM ALL. INFECTED THEM WITH HIS EVIL.

"ONCE I HAD PUT MY BELOVED ELOWEN'S SOUL TO REST ONCE MORE, I SET AFTER THEM.

"THEY HADN'T GONE FAR."

THERE WILL BE NO BLOOD FOR YOU TONIGHT.

HRR

YOU WEAR MY SISTER'S FACE, BUT YOU ARE NOT SHE.

ABOMINATION.

HSSSSSSSS

KLANKK

OH, NO. PLEASE.

PLEASE, HENRY, SET ME FREE! CAN'T YOU SEE IT'S ME? IT'S HELEN.

123

"...I WANT TO GO HOME.

"YOU ARE A GOOD MAN, LORD BALTIMORE. BUT MY GRANDMOTHER WAS RIGHT...YOU ARE CURSED. *DAMNED.*

"I WOULD FEAR FOR MY SOUL WERE I TO REMAIN WITH YOU.

"AND I DO NOT WANT YOU TO HAVE TO REMEMBER ME WITH A HAMMER AND A NAIL.

"NO, LORD BALTIMORE, IT'S BEST I RETURN TO VILLEFRANCHE...

"THE VILLAGE MAY BE A RUIN, BUT AT LEAST A SPARK OF LIFE AND HOPE ENDURES. I CAN HAVE A LIFE THERE, WITH MY GRANDMOTHER.
"AT HOME, AT LEAST I WILL BE SAFE."
AAIIIEEEE
...
I AM THE INQUISITION, WITCH. I KNOW YOU ARE IN LEAGUE WITH VAMPIRES.
YOU WILL BEAR THE MARK OF YOUR EVIL FOR ALL YOUR DAYS. BUT THOSE DAYS END NOW, UNLESS YOU SPEAK TRUE.
TELL ME EVERYTHING YOU KNOW OF THE ONE WHO CALLS HIMSELF LORD BALTIMORE.
THE END

BALTIMORE
THE PLAGUE SHIPS

SKETCHBOOK

Notes by Ben Stenbeck

Some early "kite" sketches. They didn't really need any design work.
Mike just wanted them to look like bats. Which is creepy enough.

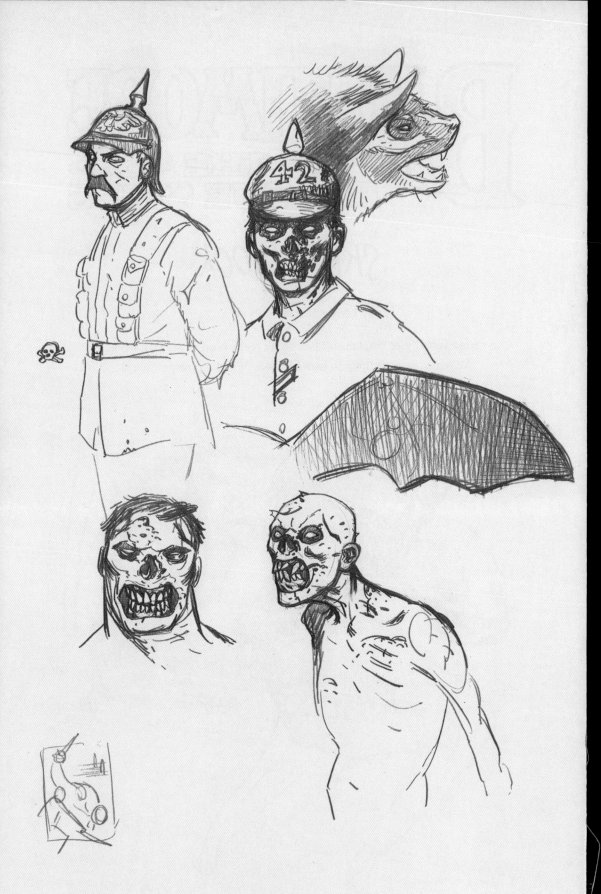

Following: new pinups done especially for this collection.

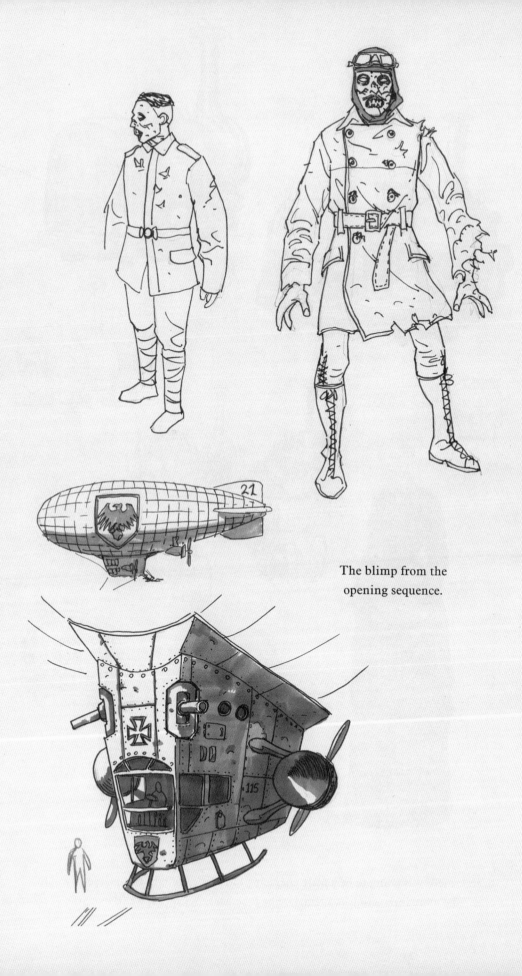

The blimp from the
opening sequence.

Fulcanelli was going to be a male character, but Mike thought the character would
be more interesting as a female. She'll be back. With that weird machine.

Jellyfish things. We decided not to go too weird on their look. And I'm looking forward to drawing more of Judge Duvic. I think this was my first sketch of Baltimore.

Beard more scruffy

straps cross / High an chest

DUVIC

BALTIMORE'S LEG

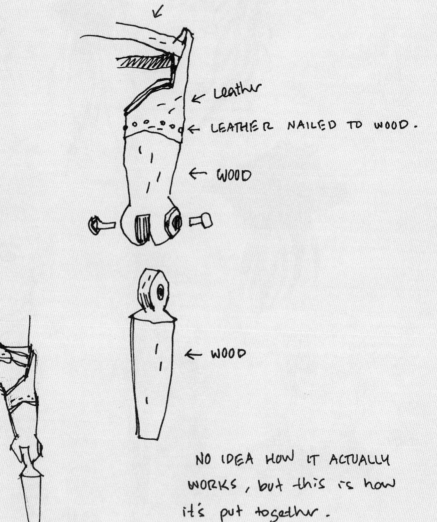

some kind of belt to go around waist under clothes?

← Leather

← LEATHER NAILED TO WOOD.

← WOOD

← WOOD

NO IDEA HOW IT ACTUALLY WORKS, but this is how it's put together.

Just as he's had to do with Hellboy's hand, Mike provides a mechanical guide for Baltimore's leg.

Layout for Page 14

Witch hand – Finger touching water in bowl .. We need this to clearly establish color (red) in water.

BLEED

Foreground misty -- Not too much detail.

Vision is behind Baltimore - Baltimore overlaps it --

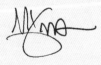

TO SCOTT ALLIE - BEN STENBECK - CHRIS GOLDEN

Page 22 was originally scripted to have more panels, but after seeing Ben's layout, Mike sent this suggestion for simplifying it. The same layout was revisited again on page 99.

—Scott Allie

Fungus-creature stuff. This was too much fun.

More preparation and design was done for the fungus
zombies than any other part of the book.

Dive suits, for doing underwater stuff. This design wasn't clunky enough.
So then I did the ones on the next page.

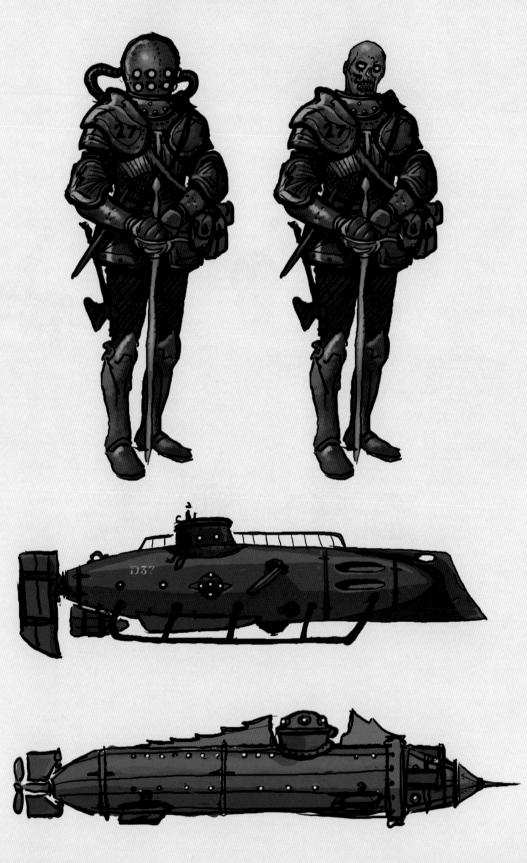

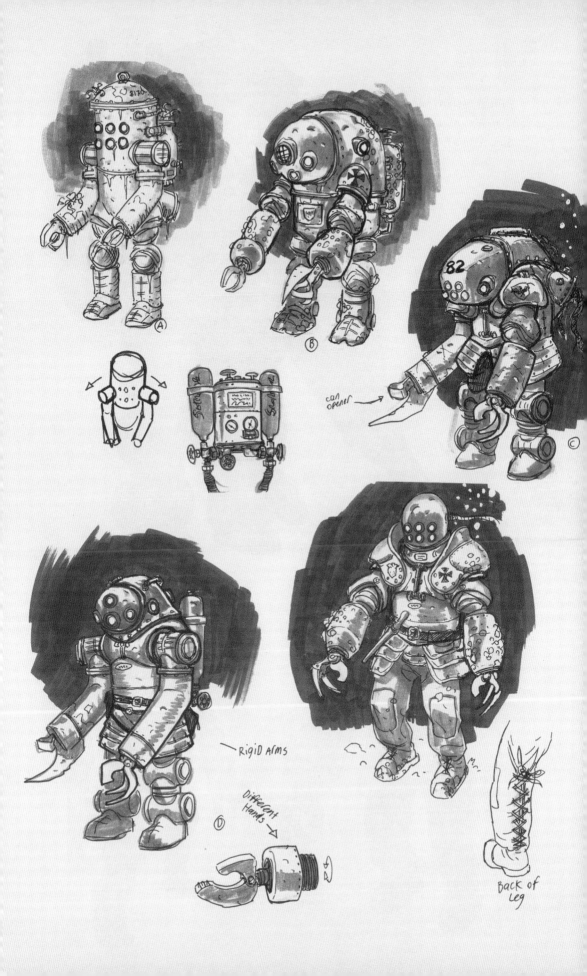

can opener

Rigid Arms

Different Hands

BACK OF LEG

Final designs and scale comparisons of the two different suits. Also a fungus zombie.